W9-ARA-228

Date: 9/28/17

J 621.988 ABE
Abell, Tracy,
All about 3D printing /

CUTTING-EDGE TECHNOLOGY

ALL ABOUT 3D PRINTING

by Tracy Abell

WWW.NORTHSTAREDITIONS.COM

Produced for North Star Editions by Red Line Editorial.

Photographs ©: vgajic/iStockphoto, cover, 1; Twinkind/Rex Features/AP Images, 4–5; Ruan Banhui/Imaginechina/AP Images, 6; Andrew Milligan/PA Wire/AP Images, 9; Mehdi Chebil/Polaris/Newscom, 10–11; Mopic/Shutterstock Images, 12; Damian Dovarganes/AP Images, 14; RAGMA IMAGES/Shutterstock Images, 16 (top left); wsf-s/Shutterstock Images, 16 (top right), 16 (bottom), 17 (top), 17 (bottom); Nikirov/Shutterstock Images, 18–19; Steve Lagreca/Shutterstock Images, 20; Alexander Tolstykh/Shutterstock Images, 22–23; science photo/Shutterstock Images, 25; Kelly Wilkinson/Indianapolis Star/AP Images, 26–27; Lin Hui/Imaginechina/AP Images, 29

Content Consultant: Dr. Howard A. Kuhn, Adjunct Professor, University of Pittsburgh

ISBN
978-1-63517-009-2 (hardcover)
978-1-63517-065-8 (paperback)
978-1-63517-170-9 (ebook pdf)
978-1-63517-120-4 (hosted ebook)

Library of Congress Control Number: 2016949754

Printed in the United States of America
Mankato, MN
November, 2016

ABOUT THE AUTHOR

Tracy Abell lives in the Rocky Mountain foothills in a house big enough for four people, two dogs, two cats, and a bunch of stuff she probably doesn't need. Her next adventure might include living in a 3D-printed tiny house near the ocean.

TABLE OF CONTENTS

CHAPTER 1

WHAT IS 3D PRINTING?

Step into the scanner booth. Now strike a pose. Whatever you do, hold still. You see a bright flash. Your picture is taken by 54 cameras at once. Special **software** turns those images into a **digital** model. Next, the software separates that model into a stack of thin slices.

A company in Germany makes detailed portraits using 3D printers.

Special software turns a series of photographs into a 3D model.

Then, a 3D printer puts down a layer of powder in the shape of the first slice.

The printer repeats this process for each slice in the model. The slices are fused together. Finally, a technician reaches into the powder. She pulls out a plastic toy. Congratulations! You are now an action figure.

3D is short for "three-dimensional." An object is 3D if it has length, width, and height. A 3D printer creates three-dimensional objects. These printers can make toys, clothes, or even jet engine parts. 3D printers form these objects by adding one layer of material at a time. That's why 3D printing is sometimes known as additive manufacturing. Some people also call it direct digital manufacturing.

There are a variety of 3D printer sizes. There are also different printer materials and printing processes to choose from. It all depends on what a person wants to create.

For example, the 3D printer that built a cement apartment building in China is very different from a printer used to create **prosthetic** arms.

3D printing began in the early 1980s. A researcher wanted to print an object using liquid plastic that would harden in layers. Several years later, his idea

RAPID PROTOTYPING

3D printing was invented as a way to quickly make prototypes. A prototype is the first model of an invention. Designers test the sample to make sure it works. If it doesn't, they make changes and print another model. Prototypes help designers get their inventions just right.

Scientists are working on ways to 3D-print organs for people with health problems.

became a reality. A 3D object was created by digital data fed into a printer. **UV laser** beams were aimed at liquid plastics. Wherever the light hit, the liquid became solid plastic.

By the 2010s, 3D printers could make jewelry, tools, vehicles, and more. The possibilities of 3D printing seem almost endless!

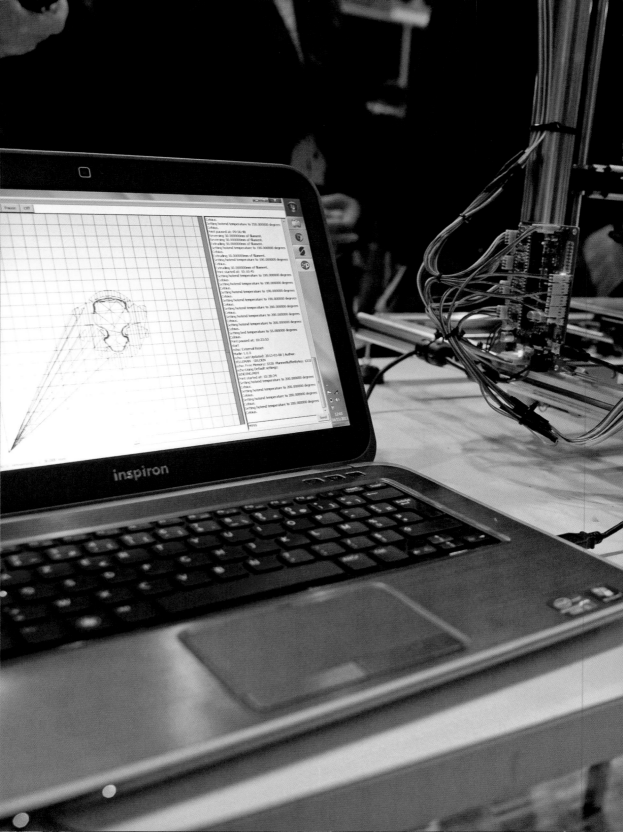

CHAPTER 2

HOW 3D PRINTERS WORK

All 3D-printed objects have one thing in common. Each starts with a design file on a computer. That file is a digital model of the object you want to print. The digital model is separated into many thin slices. The design file tells the printer the precise shape of each slice in the object.

A digital file tells the 3D printer what to make.

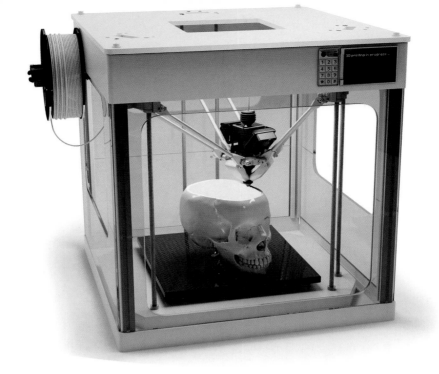

Each printed slice is extremely thin, giving the object a smooth appearance.

As all of these slices are printed on top of one another, the object forms its 3D shape.

3D printers fall into four main categories. These are based on the types of materials used. The first kind of printer uses **photopolymers**. A build platform is barely lowered into a vat of liquid photopolymers. The design file tells the printer where to pass a laser over the thin layer of liquid. Everywhere the laser shines, it turns the liquid into solid plastic. When that layer is complete, the platform is lowered a tiny bit. Again, the laser passes over certain parts of the liquid and makes it solid. This process is repeated until the object is complete.

Another kind of printer uses layers of powder. That powder must be turned into a solid. There are different ways to do this. One method involves spraying glue in the powder. Another method fuses the powder together with a laser.

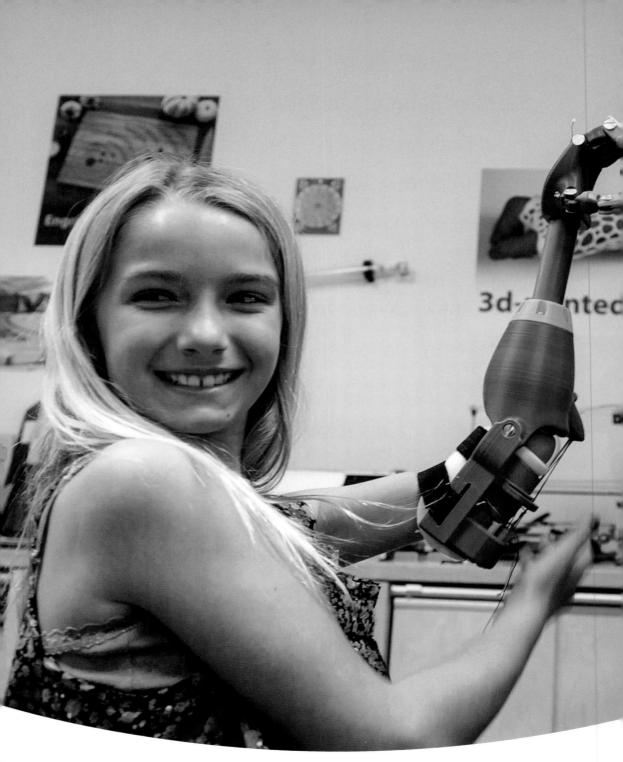

 A girl uses a prosthetic hand made with a 3D printer.

A third type of printer uses rolls of material. These include plastic sheets, metal foils, and paper. The material is rolled across the build platform. The printer cuts out the shape for each slice. Each cut-out slice is combined using heat and glue.

The most popular type of everyday 3D printer uses plastic **filament**. The filament is melted and comes out of a nozzle, similar to toothpaste from a tube. Each slice cools quickly, and the next slice is added.

CLOSE-UP OF A 3D PRINTER

1. The printer receives a computer design file.

2. Plastic thread unwinds from a spool. The plastic is fed through a nozzle.

3. The nozzle melts the plastic. That plastic is released onto the build platform. The computer file tells the nozzle where to move.

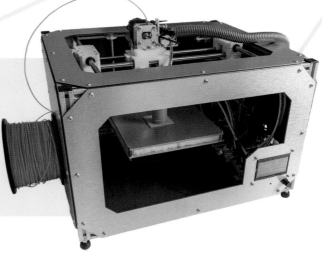

4. After the first slice is finished, the platform drops lower. The next slice is added.

5. The printer continues adding slices until the object is complete.

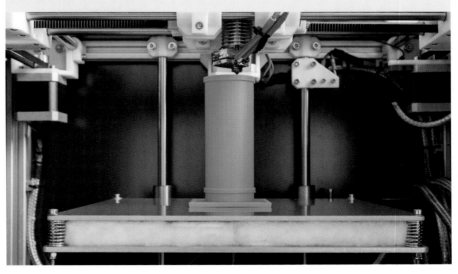

Note: As with all 3D printers, the object being printed cannot be bigger than the printer.

CHAPTER 3

WHAT CAN 3D PRINTERS DO?

Some printers create tiny objects. One person built a working power drill that was only 0.67 inches (1.7 cm) tall. Another person used a huge printer to build a concrete castle in his backyard. A college student who couldn't afford regular braces created **nontoxic** plastic braces on a 3D printer at his school.

A large 3D printer creates a building out of cement.

This 3D-printed car was created by a company called Local Motors.

In 2014, a company produced the world's first 3D-printed car.

3D printers can also make replacement parts. The US Navy has 3D printers on some of its ships. When parts are lost or broken, the crew prints new ones. A company in France wants customers to be able to fix their own appliances. The company provides free online plans. Customers with access to 3D printers can print out oven knobs and vacuum hoses.

3D printers are also used in schools. Some printers are used to create drones and robots for less money than it costs to buy them. Other printers make models of human organs for students to study. 3D printers can also create **topographic maps**. Some classrooms even use 3D printers to print out prosthetics. They team up with a global organization called e-NABLE. The organization matches people who need prosthetics with owners of 3D printers.

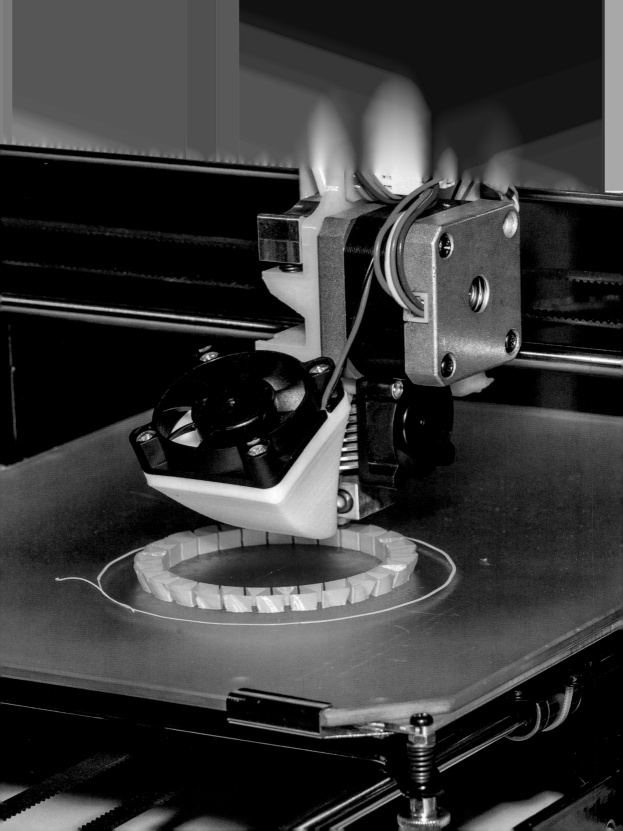

CHAPTER 4

POTENTIAL PROBLEMS

3D printing is an exciting technology. It's fun to watch an idea transform into something you can hold in your hands. But as more people use 3D printers, more plastic junk will end up in landfills. Also, plastic causes air pollution when it melts.

Plastic is made from oil, which is a fossil fuel.

There are also safety concerns. Most plastics used in 3D printing are not safe for contact with food or drink. Also, items that are printed and sold may not be safety tested. For example, who is responsible if a 3D-printed bike helmet fails? And what happens if a person prints dangerous objects?

"GREEN" 3D PRINTING

Markus Kayser figured out a way to 3D-print without electricity or toxic plastic. He put sand in a special box and used a lens to aim the sun at it. The sun fused the sand into glass. A solar panel powered the printer to move the lens. Kayser created bowls using 100-percent renewable energy and sand.

As technology advances, engineers may develop filaments that are more environmentally friendly.

To help minimize environmental problems, some people make their own filaments. They do so by recycling plastic parts made by others. They chop up the parts into small pieces, melt the pieces, and create new filament.

CHAPTER 5

THE FUTURE OF 3D PRINTING

The price of 3D printers keeps dropping. Over time, more and more people will own one. More printers will be available at public libraries and **makerspaces**. People could begin designing items for themselves. They might make their own clothes. Athletic gear and shoes could be custom-fitted.

A dog that was born with only two legs uses a customized cart made with a 3D printer.

Someday, 3D printers could make food. Scientists are working on 3D-printed pizzas for astronauts to eat during long space missions. Others are working to invent 3D-printed hamburgers made from lab-grown meat cells.

INTELLECTUAL PROPERTY

Intellectual property (IP) is anything a person creates in his or her mind. One issue with 3D printing is keeping track of who invented what. Design files are often uploaded to the web. But if someone changes the file and then sells that changed design, who owns the IP rights? The 3D printing industry is searching for ways to protect designers' IP rights.

This 3D printer is designed to make pancakes.

The 3D printing process itself will also go through changes. More printing materials will be widely available. One possible type of filament is called shrilk. It is made from shrimp shells and silkworm fibers. Shrilk is nontoxic, so it is food-safe and better for the planet.

FOCUS ON
3D PRINTING

Write your answers on a separate piece of paper.

1. Write a sentence that summarizes the key ideas of Chapter 2.

2. Do you think 3D printing has more potential benefits or potential problems? Why?

3. What is shrilk made from?
   - **A.** gold powder
   - **B.** shrimp shells
   - **C.** plastic

4. Why might plastic filament be a bad choice for a 3D-printed spoon?
   - **A.** because the plastic may not be strong enough
   - **B.** because the plastic may not be food-safe
   - **C.** because the plastic may not be the right color

Answer key on page 32.

GLOSSARY

digital
Having to do with information used on a computer.

filament
A thin thread.

laser
A powerful beam of light.

makerspaces
Places where people gather to invent and create together.

nontoxic
Not poisonous.

photopolymers
Special kinds of plastic that can change from liquid to solid when a certain kind of light shines on them.

prosthetic
Having to do with artificial body parts.

software
The programs that run on a computer and perform certain functions.

topographic maps
Maps that show the heights and depths of an area.

UV
Abbreviation for ultraviolet; a type of invisible light.

TO LEARN MORE

BOOKS

Marcovitz, Hal. *3-D Printing*. Chicago: Norwood House Press, 2016.

Murphy, Maggie. *High-Tech DIY Projects with 3D Printing*. New York: PowerKids Press, 2015.

O'Neill, Terence, and Josh Williams. *3D Printing*. Ann Arbor, MI: Cherry Lake Publishing, 2013.

NOTE TO EDUCATORS

Visit **www.focusreaders.com** to find lesson plans, activities, links, and other resources related to this title.

INDEX

Answer Key: **1.** Answers will vary; **2.** Answers will vary; **3.** B; **4.** B